...But, what If...

Copyright © 2020 Erica N. Wortherly, LCSW

First Edition

All rights reserved.

This book, or parts thereof, may not be reproduced in any form without permission from the publisher. Exceptions are made for brief excerpts used in published reviews.

ISBN 978-1933518-45-9

Printed in the United States of America

# ...But, what If...

Written by Erica N. Wortherly

Illustrated by Daniella & Yanelie Lott

## A Note to Adults...

This book is intended to be read with a child or group of children to facilitate a discussion about anxiety. When someone faces potentially harmful or worrying triggers, feelings of anxiety are not only normal but necessary for survival. This can appear as a 'fight-freeze-flight' reaction. Anxieties *can* occur when thinking about work/school, money, family life, health, and other critical issues that demand a person's attention without causing the 'fight-freeze-flight' reaction. The nervous feeling, or butterflies, before an important event or during a challenging situation is a natural parallel of the 'fight-freeze-flight' reaction. Anxiety about being in a car accident, for example, means that a person will instinctively check surroundings to avoid danger.

Most children are ready to explore their world. Many children have fears and worries. Strong fears may appear at different times during development. Parents and other adults tend to teach fear; though usually not on purpose, the fear response in children becomes a learned behavior.

Anxiety may look like fear or worry, but can also make children irritable and angry. Consider the following:

- Be mindful of your responses to worry and fear. What are you modeling for this child?
- Create healthy boundaries, yet allow room for exploration.
- Help the child face fears.
- Praise the child for efforts to cope with fears and worry.
- Help the child talk about feelings.
- Listen and let them know you understand, love, and accept them. A caring relationship with you helps the child build inner strengths.
- Encourage and help the child to take small, positive steps forward. Don't let the child give up or avoid what they're afraid of if the situation is not harmful.
- Find a therapist and communicate often to determine the best way for you to help the child, if needed.

*To the children who are nervous about the unknown.*

*You are not alone.*

*Bringing light to those who are afraid of what comes next.*

What if...
...Nobody wants to play with me
...I don't say the right thing
...They don't like the way I look
...I fail that quiz I took

...But, what if I am a part of the team ...I know more than I think.

Nobody is perfect, and I know you want everything to work out perfectly. This is not reality. If we are not sure how things will turn out, we do worry.

That feeling is called anxiety. When we are doing something new or different this is a normal feeling. If you are performing, especially for the first time, it can be hard not to think about making a mistake or what people might say.

What if...
...I disappoint my family
...They stop loving me
...I can't make friends
...And I'm alone in the end?

...But, what if they surround me with care ...at least one person is always there?

Sometimes, anxiety is a part of who you are because you are more cautious than others.

Sometimes, when you see other people worry a lot, they teach you to worry.

Sometimes, someone in your family has anxiety, so you have it too.

Sometimes, you think the worst to prepare for the worst.

what if...
...The storm comes this way
...we don't have a place to stay
...I get sick or hurt
...someone doesn't get better

*...But, what if my needs and wants are met ...we will be okay and make the most of it?*

Anxiety, fear, and worry help you:

- slow down when you need to take your time,
- move away from things it is smart to avoid,
- run or fight if the danger is real.

Your stomach may ache. Your body may tense up like a statue. Your heart can begin pounding. It may be hard to breathe.

what if...
...I'm not good enough
...I can't be strong and tough
...Nobody cares for me
...I can't put my mind at ease

*...But, what if I believe in myself ...I put my doubt on the shelf*

You are very creative. You can imagine all kinds of problems that can be scary even if they never happen. "What if..." questions can take over your mind when you don't know the answers.

what if...
...I get in trouble
...This is uncomfortable
...My fears are real
...I can't stop the way they make feel

Anxiety and worry will not disappear, it is a part of who you are. There are ways to keep that voice from taking you on a ride you want to get off of. Be willing to be uncomfortable. Your brain will come up with ways to get you through.

# BUT...

what if...
...I see that I am not alone
...I do not fear the unknown
...I get the help I need
...I use the power inside me

You are human after all.

All humans have emotions.

All emotions work together and help you know who you are. You are strong and special.

The anxiety you feel is there to protect you.

Take a deep breath and notice the good in your life.

**A**ttitude-Mindset is key to problem-solving. Being flexible and open-minded reduces feelings of fear.

**N**atural-It is normal to fear the unknown. It is also normal to be curious.

**X**-tra sleep.-Get a good night's sleep to help your mental, emotional and physical health.

**I**nvestigate-Asking, 'what is happening inside me?' and answering that question can help you understand how your mind works.

**E**xercise-Physical fitness can actually help you calm down. It gives your nervous energy a place to go.

**T**ry-Even if it does not work out the first time, or second, or third, do it again. You will learn, and it can get better.

**Y**es-It's okay to say "Yes" to things that might be scary. It could be a fun, new experience or create a fantastic memory.

# ...But, what if...
## Addressing Anxiety

What if...(Social)
...Nobody wants to play with me
...I don't say the right thing
...They don't like the way I look
...I fail that quiz I took

What if...(Relational)
...I disappoint my family
...They stop loving me
...I can't make friends
...And I'm alone in the end

What if...(Physical)
...The storm comes this way
...We don't have a place to stay
...I get sick or hurt
...They don't get better

What if...(Mental)
...I'm not good enough
...I can't be strong and tough
...Nobody cares for me
...I can't put my mind at ease

What if...(Emotional)
...I get in trouble
...This is uncomfortable
...My fears are real
...I can't stop the way they make me feel

BUT...

What if...(Resilience)
...I see that I am not alone
...I do not fear the unknown
...I get the help I need
...I use the power inside me

# Coping Skills & Activities

- Expression
- Physical Activity
- Mindfulness/Grounding
- Exposure

*All your feelings are natural; it is what you do when you are feeling that way that makes the difference.*

# Expression

**Benefits**

There are many forms of expression to communicate emotions. You are an individual and, like all situations, you will not respond the same as others. Your personality and process should be respected and nurtured. Challenge what you think. When a bad thought comes in, find a way to flip it to something better.

**Tips**
- Talk with a trusted adult.
- Ask questions.
- Understand your triggers.
- List what you can control vs. what you can't.
- Discuss memories and how things turned out.
- Talk about dreams and goals.
- Keep a daily routine.
- Practice random acts of kindness.
- Write a story.
- Write in a journal.
- Draw or paint.

# Physical Activity

**Benefits**

Movement can help you use your energy. When you are feeling difficult emotions, you can have bursts of energy running through your body. Sometimes, you will not want to move at all. Moving can help change your mood and help you to feel better.

**Tips**
- Play.
- Swing.
- Go for a walk or run.
- Squeeze something, a pillow or stress ball.
- Hold a small stone.
- Make up a game.
- Stretch.
- Dance.
- Clean.

# Mindfulness/Grounding

**Benefits**

Mindfulness is being aware of what is happening in the present moment, not focusing on the past or the future. It can be done anywhere. Grounding is a way to deal with overwhelming emotions. The goal of these types of exercises is to get from "fight, flight, or freeze" mode back to "rest and digest" mode. Use these when you need to be brought back to the present moment.

**Tips**
- Breathe in through your nose and expand the belly, then breathe out slowly. This could also be practiced with balloons, bubbles, or a pinwheel.
- Imagine your favorite place.
- Mental grounding is thinking of your favorite things, picturing people you care about, saying the alphabet slowly (forward or backwards), or remembering the words to a song you love. It could also be going through the five senses to help remind you of the present; paying attention to what you can see, feel, hear, smell, and taste.
- Physical grounding is running water in your hands, carrying a small object like a stone or shell, tightening and releasing different parts of your body.

# Exposure

**Benefits**

The more you know, the more you can use what you know to cope. Trying new experiences helps you learn that life may not be as scary as you think. It shows you that if you can look beyond the anxiety, you can feel happiness, peace and enjoy life!

**Tips**
- Take risks and do some of the things that cause you to be afraid. Ask yourself why it is scary or makes you nervous. Do this with someone you trust and share your thoughts and feelings.
- Face fears one at a time.
- Understand the difference between do vs. do well. If you are doing something for the first time, be patient. You can get better.
- If you don't think you can, you can't. Keep trying.

But, what if I get the help I need.

And what if I use the power inside me.

**Erica N. Wortherly** specializes in working with educators and parents to improve their understanding of mental health. She travels for speaking engagements in schools, churches and conferences for professional development and caregiver workshops on topics including: self-care practices, mental health awareness, personality differences, and more.

As a former teacher and social worker, she will always be an educator. Erica advocates for shifting mindsets to create more flexible, empathetic and comfortable environments for children and the adults who care for them to thrive.

For more information about Erica N. Wortherly or to order more copies of *...But, What If...* and other books, please visit www.ericanwortherly.com.

~ ~ ~

**Daniella and Yanelie Lott** are twin sisters who are high school students majoring in Visual Arts at Douglas Anderson School of the Arts in Jacksonville, FL. Daniella's major is sculpture. She loves to see the outcome of shaping and molding a lump of clay into a work of art. Yanelie's major is painting. She is able to capture the most minute details and her images come to life with the stroke of her paint brush. At any given time, you may see either one of them with their head down, pencil in hand, sketching away and seemingly effortlessly producing reflections of what they see or imagine on the pages of their sketchbooks. Follow them at Facebook.com/AwesomeX2VisualArts/

www.ingramcontent.com/pod-product-compliance
Lightning Source LLC
Chambersburg PA
CBHW081800100526
44592CB00015B/2508